Goddess Reveals
Your Enchanted Light
Peace, Prosperity, Possibility
Along Your Wiccan Path

from GoddessHasYourBack.com

Moonwater SilverClaw

Wiccan High Priestess

Blogger/Founder of

GoddessHasYourBack.com

with visitors from **173 countries**

A QuickBreakthrough Publishing Edition

More copies are available from the publisher with the imprint QuickBreakthrough Publishing. For more information about this book contact: askawitchnow@gmail.com

This book was developed and written with care. Names and details were modified to respect privacy.

Disclaimer: The author and publisher acknowledge that each person's situation is unique, and that readers have full responsibility to seek consultations with health, financial, spiritual and legal professionals. The author and publisher make no representations or warranties of any kind, and the author and publisher shall not be liable for any special, consequential or exemplary damages resulting, in whole or in part, from the reader's use of, or reliance upon, this material.:

Other Books by Moonwater SilverClaw:
- Goddess Has Your Back
- Goddess Walks Beside You
- The Hidden Children of the Goddess
- Beyond the Law of Attraction to Real Magick

Praise for Moonwater SilverClaw:

• "In her book *The Hidden Children of the Goddess*, Moonwater brings Wicca to life, enveloping you in the mystery and magick of the Craft. Her writing talent is amazing! Her kindness and even sense of fun is ever present throughout her writing. Moonwater expresses profound Wicca concepts through examples in her own life experience. Wicca actually saved her life. and empowered her to leave an abusive marriage, and this shows the power of this sacred path to positively change the course of our lives, too. Moonwater's stories personally inspire me, and I am confident that they will inspire you also." – Rev. Patrick McCollum, internationally recognized spiritual leader working for human rights, social justice, and equality; the 2010 recipient of the Mahatma Gandhi Award for the Advancement of Pluralism.

• "Religion scholars in the future will likely view Moonwater SilverClaw as the pivotal voice that helped change the discourse on Wicca. In her book **Goddess Has Your Back,** Moonwater reveals Wicca as a very positive and ultimately uplifting spirituality choice. She demystifies the religion's taboos and spooky stereotypes through her unintimidating presentation that clarifies the topic. She introduces the Goddess and the magick rituals that, when used properly, can positively impact your everyday life. The author relays her very personal perspective on the subject and shows how to integrate the philosophies and practices of the centuries-old religion. Looking for a fresh perspective on spiritual growth? Read what Moonwater SilverClaw has to say. She may very well point you in the direction where you need to go." – Stacy D. Horn

• "Moonwater's writing will give you a portrait of a woman who lives her faith, and whose life was saved by it. Because so many lives, my own included, were irrevocably changed by Wicca, were given new focus, new purpose, and perhaps most importantly, new personal power to realize one's dreams and ambitions. . . . It's a story about making your own happy endings, about rescuing yourself, and that, I believe, is what makes writing like this necessary." – Jason Pitzl-Waters, blogger at WildHunt.org

Visit Moonwater's blog: www.GoddessHasYourBack.com

CONTENTS*

* This table has highlights. Much more material is in this book!

DEDICATION AND ACKNOWLEDGEMENTS

This book is dedicated to the God and Goddess. Thanks to Tom Marcoux for editing. Thanks to Kay Pannell for her guidance and friendship.

CHAPTER ONE

GODDESS REVEALS
YOUR ENCHANTED LIGHT

Have you felt the presence of the Goddess? I have. I know that connecting with the Goddess can help you during good times and bad.

In recent years, I've learned something even more powerful:

Goddess Reveals Your Enchanted Light!

What does this mean? I had to learn about this on my own path. When I was younger, I was emotionally shutdown; certain terrible things had slammed me. Darkness was my world.

But then I met the Goddess and the God and They showed me that I have an inner light and an inner strength.

Since that time, it's been my journey to encourage other people so they can see *their* light.

I'm grateful that we're connecting through this book. Think of me as a new friend having coffee with you. We're going to talk about real blessings you can come to know. For example ...

SECRET #1: Goddess Wants You To Feel the Divine Connection with Her

As Wiccans, we celebrate that we have been given the knowledge to access our inner divinity. Additionally, we can "raise up natural power."

How do we do that? Through our spellwork.

For you to really experience Your Enchanted Light, it helps for you to become extra skillful in your spellwork ...

Nurture Your Enchanted Light #1

When A Spell Doesn't Work; Use the Power of Customizing Your Spell

"My spell didn't work," Anne told me. Then, she explained how she did the steps exactly in the manner that someone's book had advised.

"I just had an intuitive thought about this," I said.

"What?"

"It seems that you really need to customize the spell in order for it to work in your life and at this moment," I said.

Spellwork really arises from you. Spells tend to be weak when you are following someone else's thoughts on what a good spell is.

So how do you create a good spell, one that truly works for you?

Follow these Three Steps of Customizing a Spell:

1. Ask: "What is it I really want to accomplish?"

What kind of spell do you want to do? What is the *work or outcome* you want? In this section, we will customize a prosperity spell.

I was working with a friend, Jim, and he said, "I want to focus on creating more prosperity in my life. I would like to see more abundance and more wealth in my life. I really need more money coming my way."

I'm glad that he said, "wealth" because it's a more useful word than "rich."

I make a distinction between the two ideas:

Rich: A state of acquiring large amounts of money but not having lots of it in reserves. In this way you can have a lot of money, but it may not be a permanent feature of your life.

Wealth: Wealth tends to be permanent. It is a state of being. You continue to have an abundance of financial resources.

I asked Jim, "How will you know when you are wealthy?"

He replied, "I'll know that I have given someone value and in response they pay me generously for my work."

"Jim, ask yourself, 'How am I going to be able to do that?' You don't need the answer now. Many times the Gods will guide you after the spell."

It's better when we shift from focusing only on money. We really need to focus on having the energy, opportunities, or knowledge to get money flowing into our lives.

I will tell you a secret. Magick changes you, and then you

change the world around you.

So spellwork when done properly is usually focused on yourself.

I know this process of working on yourself brings great results. You see, you're not asking for a handout. For example, I received thousands of dollars by developing myself and becoming more capable as a person. The Gods like it when you work on yourself.

Let's continue.

2. What element(s) do you want to work with?

I like Fire because it is a transformative element. It changes one thing into another. Also the smoke from the sacred flame will go up to the Gods so they can help with your need. Sending up smoke sends a clear message to the Gods and Goddesses of what you want and why. We will use a green candle to carry the sacred flame to transform your need into a blessing that manifests in reality.

3. Putting it all together.

The first part of putting it all together is to identify the proper moon phase, time and day for prosperity work.

Moon Phase

Many Wiccans make a big mistake of failing to look at the moon phase before doing a spell. Because Sara (someone I know) didn't look at the moon when she did her prosperity spell, she missed the vital detail that the moon was waning. That's a problem because the waning moon is for decreasing work. She did *not* want her income to decrease!

What could Sara have done to have *more money* in her purse? She could have done a spell to *decrease* the size of her bills.

The truth is: You can do many spells at any time *if you word the spell correctly.*

As many Wiccans know, the waxing moon is for increase so it would have been better if Sara waited for the waxing moon if she wanted to stay with the original form of her prosperity spell.

Days of the Week

Another strategy for making your spell more potent is to use the correct day of the week. Plan to do your spell on the day that *rules* what you are seeking to accomplish. Here is an abbreviated list of the days, Deities and what they rule.

Sunday – Helios – Prosperity, power, strength, vitality, honor, passion

Monday – Diana – Agriculture, childbirth, instinct, a woman's cycles, secrets

Tuesday – Mars – Conflict resolution, drive, war, domination, justice, protection

Wednesday – Mercury – intellect, communication, mind and intellectual pursuits, law and court cases

Thursday – Jupiter – Travel, wisdom, animals, gambling, increase

Friday – Venus – Love spells, feminine issues, emotions, marriage

Saturday – Saturn – Discipline, responsibility, hard work

Planetary Hours

The next thing you can do to power up your spell is perform your spell at the correct hour.

Planetary Hours of the Day

Hour	Sunday	Monday	Tuesday	Wednesday	Thursday	Friday	Saturday
1	Sun	Moon	Mars	Mercury	Jupiter	Venus	Saturn
2	Venus	Saturn	Sun	Moon	Mars	Mercury	Jupiter
3	Mercury	Jupiter	Venus	Saturn	Sun	Moon	Mars
4	Moon	Mars	Mercury	Jupiter	Venus	Saturn	Sun
5	Saturn	Sun	Moon	Mars	Mercury	Jupiter	Venus
6	Jupiter	Venus	Saturn	Sun	Moon	Mars	Mercury
7	Mars	Mercury	Jupiter	Venus	Saturn	Sun	Moon
8	Sun	Moon	Mars	Mercury	Jupiter	Venus	Saturn
9	Venus	Saturn	Sun	Moon	Mars	Mercury	Jupiter
10	Mercury	Jupiter	Venus	Saturn	Sun	Moon	Mars
11	Moon	Mars	Mercury	Jupiter	Venus	Saturn	Venus
12	Saturn	Sun	Moon	Mars	Mercury	Jupiter	Mercury

Planetary Hours of the Night

Hour	Sunday	Monday	Tuesday	Wednesday	Thursday	Friday	Saturday
1	Jupiter	Venus	Saturn	Sun	Moon	Mars	Mercury
2	Mars	Mercury	Jupiter	Venus	Saturn	Sun	Moon
3	Sun	Moon	Mars	Mercury	Jupiter	Venus	Saturn
4	Venus	Saturn	Sun	Moon	Mars	Mercury	Jupiter
5	Mercury	Jupiter	Venus	Saturn	Sun	Moon	Mars
6	Moon	Mars	Mercury	Jupiter	Venus	Saturn	Sun
7	Saturn	Sun	Moon	Mars	Mercury	Jupiter	Venus
8	Jupiter	Venus	Saturn	Sun	Moon	Mars	Mercury
9	Mars	Mercury	Jupiter	Venus	Saturn	Sun	Moon
10	Sun	Moon	Mars	Mercury	Jupiter	Venus	Saturn
11	Venus	Saturn	Sun	Moon	Mars	Mercury	Jupiter
12	Mercury	Jupiter	Venus	Saturn	Sun	Moon	Mars

Supercharge your spellwork by adding the correct moon phase, day and planetary hour. Using these strategies adds energy to your spell. Such energy helps your intention, through your spellwork, find its mark.

The next step is to write your own short set of phrases.

You might want to attempt to write a rhyme.

Warning: Include in your words details that ensure that the situation "harms none"! You want to make sure that no one is hurt in the process of getting more money to you. You don't want your favorite aunt (or yourself!) to get in a car accident—for example.

Your next step is to add the little touches like money oil. Soon you'll have your customized spell.

Money Spell

You will need:
- A green candle
- Boline
- A Check from the Universe [You write this out addressed to you—with the memo "For the good of all" And sign it "The Universe."]
- Cauldron
- Money drawing oil
- Money Oil (add drops of essential oils together)
- 3 parts ginger
- 2 parts orange
- 4 parts pine
- 2 parts cinnamon
- 1/2 part chamomile
- 1 part cedar wood
- 5 parts jasmine (optional)
- matches or a lighter

WARNING: This spell should be worked *only* during the waxing moon.

Cast circle in the usual manner. Take the green candle and carve your name onto it. Then dress the candle with the money oil envisioning money flowing into your life. (To dress the candle, you apply oil from the top to the center of the candle—and from the bottom to the center of the candle.)

Place the green candle on the altar. Direct all your energy (that you raise) to the candle say:

I summon, stir and call you up, old and ancient powers of the Sun, Moon and stars!

I summon, stir and call you up, old and ancient powers of the planets Mars, Venues and Jupiter!

I summon, stir and call you up, old and ancient powers of the planets Saturn, Mercury and Pluto!

I summon, stir and call you up, old and ancient powers of the North, South, East and West!

I summon, stir and call you up, old and ancient powers of the elements Earth, Air, Fire and Water!

I evoke you and will you to place upon me through this candle your strong powers of light and good, so that I can fulfill my needs and desires.

And that this magick will work for good and will repel all ill luck and disasters from me and all involved!

I __YOUR NAME__ will this so! So mote is be!

Next, light "The Check from the Universe," using the candle's flame and place it in the cauldron to burn safely. Watch the flame as it burns the Check from the Universe.

Meditate on the green candle's flame.

Let the green candle burn completely down. (Even after your spell, do not leave the green candle unattended while it burns.)

Enjoy the Cakes and Wine Ceremony

* * * * * *

The above was a demonstration of customizing a prosperity spell.

Goddess Reveals Your Enchanted Light
Nurture Your Enchanted Light #2

How to Raise Your Low Self-esteem Through Wicca

"How can I let go of the feelings of sadness and low self-esteem?" Alexandra asked.

I've talked with many people who, like me, suffer from times of low self-esteem.

Here is a meditation to help those of us who need to raise our self-esteem.

Find a nice quiet spot, somewhere you will *not* be disturbed. Light a candle and burn some incense if you like. Turn off all of your electronics, and get comfortable.

In the below meditation, you will identify a worn, harmful belief. Then you will represent such a Harmful Belief as one "difficult-word." For example, if your word is "can't" — soon you will place it in the fire (in your mind's eye). It will transform. For example, "can't" can transform into "I CAN learn what I need to learn." This is a New Belief.

Meditation to Raise Your Self-Esteem

Close your eyes. Be aware of the light that is in the room through your closed eyelids.

Breathe in and out deeply ... Relax.
Keep breathing deeply. In ... and ... Out.
Breathe out the stress of the day.
Breathe in relaxation and peace.

(Pause)

You are still aware of the light that is in the room.
Now the light begins to fade.
As it fades you feel total comfort. You feel safe and secure in the darkness.

(Short Pause)

Now, a new form of light blossoms around you.
You look down and see a cauldron.
Flames are fluttering from within the cauldron, and they rise to about four inches above the lip of the cauldron.

Pick one thought or memory of sadness or "I can't do it." Now identify a word that represents the difficult thought. See how the "difficult-word" appears to break down.

The difficult-word is now old and worn out.
You know in your heart that you no longer need the word.
It is time to let it go.

(Pause)

See your difficult-word. The flames in the cauldron
are flickering behind your difficult-word.
Now with your mind, push the difficult-word into the
flames.
The difficult-word catches fire, and the fire completely
consumes the difficult-word.

(Pause)

The difficult-word disappears and soon a green colored
smoke rises from the cauldron.
It starts to form your New Belief—which is in the form
of a sentence.
This New Belief helps you and supports you.
Breathe in deeply and absorb the green, supportive New
Belief.

(Pause)

The New Belief is now part of you, and you have gained
its attributes.
Feel it. Know it is so.
You now return to the physical world, and you always
know you have that positive attribute no matter what
anyone says.

(Pause)

Coming back is a gentle transition as the light begins to
fade around you once more.

**Slowly at first, it gets darker and darker.
As it fades you feel total comfort. You feel safe and
secure in the darkness.**

(Short Pause)

**Then a familiar light returns, the light in the room
where you started.
It gradually gets brighter and brighter.
You are back in the room. You have brought the feelings
of higher self-esteem and happiness back with you.**

(Short Pause)

Now, gently open your eyes.

Use the above meditation as often as you need to. With a
lot of practice, soon all of the bad thoughts about yourself
can transform into the green smoke of renewal and higher
self-esteem.

Goddess Reveals Your Enchanted Light
Nurture Your Enchanted Light #3

An Example of a Path
as Goddess Reveals Your Enchanted Light

How does Goddess truly reveal our Enchanted Light? I'll now share my journey in terms of learning about my animal Spirit Guide.

I first had a glimpse that my animal guide is a jaguar when I participated in a meditation at PantheaCon.

In my meditation, I transitioned to the astral plane. A figure stepped toward me out of the mist. I immediately recognized him as a jaguar. The energy that he radiated was "Greetings. I am your friend." He did not speak words—it was more about feelings.

Soon we traveled on the astral plane. We approached a mirror—this was a transition point to the Land of the Dead.

The jaguar surprised me because his spots then melted into total darkness, and his form transitioned to look like a dark-hued panther.

The mirror was nine feet across. My Spirit Guide and I walked through the mirror simultaneously. At my side, he served as my protector in the Land of the Dead.

When we were done, we returned to the mundane world. As I write this my Spirit Guide is here. I don't think about him, all the time. It's true that my sweetheart cannot see him. Still, I can open up my senses and know that my Spirit Guide is here.

Soon after my experience with my jaguar-Spirit Guide, I had the opportunity to see a live jaguar in Mexico. From Mexico, I brought back jaguar photos, a jaguar towel and a jaguar plush toy.

As soon as I returned from Mexico, my mind revealed a design for a jaguar tattoo. Over a course of six months and many tattoo sessions, I now have a compelling image of a jaguar on my left leg.

My point in sharing the above details is that Goddess gives you opportunities. It's like she gives you hints. It's up to each of us to welcome the possibilities and step forward with faith that Goddess guides our steps.

Goddess Reveals Your Enchanted Light
Nurture Your Enchanted Light #4

Money, Prosperity and Wiccans Enjoying Life: A Money Spell

In a gathering of friends, some conversation about money arose. You could see it. Some of the people gathered bristled.

I like to talk about prosperity which includes an abundance of love, friends, things we need and the ability to be generous.

For example, just last night, a homeless man stood outside a 7-Eleven convenience store. He asked, "Could you buy me something to drink?"

"Sure," I said. I was buying a Big Gulp, and I bought him one, too.

"Thank you," he said, quietly.

I was grateful that I had the cash in my pocket to buy something for both of us.

Sometimes, we simply need cash to buy something for another person or to pay our bills.

In light of that, here is a Money Spell.

Money Spell

You will need:

- A green candle
- "A check to yourself from the Universe"*
- Cauldron

Money Oil (add drops of essential oils together)
- 3 parts ginger
- 2 parts orange
- 4 parts pine
- 2 parts cinnamon
- 1/2 part chamomile
- 1 part cedar wood
- 5 parts jasmine (optional)
- matches or a lighter

We create a check from the Universe by writing the amount we want and writing "from the Universe for the Good of All" in the memo section on the check.

Warning: ONLY work this spell during the waxing moon.

Cast Circle in the usual manner.

Dress the green candle properly. (That is, dab your finger in the money oil and rub the candle repeatedly from wick to base—until the whole candle is covered in money oil.)

As you dress the candle, envision money flowing into your life.

Light the candle and chant the following out loud:

As I light this candle so,
Make my money grow and grow,
Let it flow without rhyme or reason,
Each and every turn of season,
Filling up my pockets so wide,
Let me enjoy this happy ride,
Make me stronger than the ocean tides,
Manifesting my will to coincide,
With no malice, woe or hitches,
May there be no mess or jinxes,
With no need of fear of ruin,
Let it rain money, bless my journey.
An it harm none, so mote it be!

Now hold the "Check from the Universe." Light the check via the candle and place the check in the cauldron to burn safely.

Watch the flame as it burns the check.

Meditate while focusing on the flame of the green candle.

When you are ready, place the green candle in a safe place and let the candle burn completely out. [Do NOT leave an untended candle. Stay safe.]

Close the Circle.

Enjoy the Cakes and Wine Ceremony

The above spell has worked for me. I had difficulty receiving appropriate checks and things cleared up. I was grateful!

May your journey be prosperous and happy.

Goddess Reveals Your Enchanted Light
Nurture Your Enchanted Light #5

Protect Yourself: Always Cast Circle

"The God of Death won't leave," I said, really concerned. My mentor nodded; she understood. This was years ago around the time of Samhain. The God of Death has many faces. The one I kept seeing was the corpse-face of a deer on a man's body.

"The God of Death wants to talk to me," I said. My mentor suggested that we do a meditation so I could find out his reason for a conversation. My mentor and I settled down in her living room, and soon I went to the astral plane to talk to the God of Death.

Once I was done and had received His message, I came back to the mundane world.

But I didn't come back alone. The God of Death clung onto me and wouldn't leave!

I ended up doing a ritual in the woods and appeased Him with a gift of a pomegranate. Finally, He left me. What a relief!

The Big Lesson

I learned something of vital importance. It's necessary for us to Cast Circle BEFORE we do a meditation.

I repeat: *Cast Circle BEFORE you do a meditation.*

In essence, I was fortunate. I learned a big lesson without having to pay a big price.

If I had Cast Circle, then the God of Death would not have returned with me from the astral plane.

Okay. Lesson learned.

Goddess Reveals Your Enchanted Light
Nurture Your Enchanted Light #6

Making the Pattern of Your Life

I'm chatting on Facebook with a distraught young woman "Janis." She has enjoyed my writing on my blog and now I'm helping her. Janis' self-esteem has been torn apart by her family members' vicious remarks about her Wiccan path.

As I help Janis, I glance at my knitting project (a blanket) at my side. It becomes so clear to me that we create our lives by the choices we make—one choice at a time.

After the Facebook chat, the conversation stays with me. I realize that every moment of my life before that Facebook chat prepared me to be in the right place at the right time. I had the right experiences so I could provide compassionate guidance for this young woman.

Imagine that your life is a knitted blanket. Each stitch represents an event or a choice you have made in life. Each time you have had an experience, you made a stitch in the blanket. The stitches including your thoughts, choices and feelings combine to make the unique fabric. So one stitch leads to another stitch and another stitch—until a blanket is made.

Then I had another thought: At the end of my life, I'll have a large, knitted blanket of experiences, thoughts and feelings. When I pass from this life do I bring the whole blanket?

Yet another thought arose. A spiritual thought. There is something that is eternal: The yarn—the essence of me. This essence continues through each project.

When we die, the pattern that we've made is like our body. We leave that behind. Soon enough, we will begin again as one single strand of yarn that will continue to manifest into the many lives during reincarnation.

When we start a new pattern; we may become a shirt or a hat this time. It all depends on what choices we make and what pattern we choose.

I find this comforting—the eternal aspect of each of us. The eternal strand of yarn.

In Wicca, I look upon reincarnation as a gift. Because we get to come back with people we loved before. In each incarnation we get to learn new stuff and make new choices. We get to have new experiences that we missed in a previous life. We get to gain spiritual wisdom in each successive incarnation.

Today I was knitting and had a mishap. I had to take apart a small section of my project. That's when I "tink" the project — yes, you're seeing the word "knit" backwards. So in knitting as with other processes in life, it's not about doing things perfectly.

It's a process. Your job is to stay aware and keep knitting, keep learning and to keep growing.

Goddess Reveals Your Enchanted Light
Nurture Your Enchanted Light #7

Listening to Our Wiccan Sisters and Brothers

Recently, I enjoyed attending PantheaCon. It was a joy to talk with people who read my blog GoddessHasYourBack.com

Recently, I was called to talk about this quote:

"Most people do not listen with the intent to understand; they listen with the intent to reply." - Stephen R. Covey

I feel that we Wiccans can feel significant pressure. Those of us who live in the continental United States of America find that we occasionally run into real prejudice!

The tough part of being in a group that is marginalized is that we lose energy and sometimes patience.

When I attend a convention, I sometimes hear arguments

among Wiccans.

I sometimes wonder: "Wait! Did they really hear what the other person said?" It seems that some individuals are so quick to take offense.

To me, Stephen R. Covey's quote points out that many of us only use listening to prepare our own argument. It's like one is listening to either tell one's side or confirm what one already believes. When we're in an argument, we do not stop to listen to the other person's feelings or thoughts. Instead, we're trying to win.

Dear Wiccan Sisters and Brothers, let's pause to hear each other out. We do not have to agree. That's the joy of being a Wiccan—we are so diverse in our beliefs and approaches.

Goddess Reveals Your Enchanted Light
Nurture Your Enchanted Light #8

How You Can Manifest Prosperity

Have you thought about how to start off the calendar New Year right? Many of us tend to make New Years resolutions. We want to manifest more prosperity in our lives. Let's avoid the first mistake in prosperity magick: tending to focus on one's outer environment verses the inner self.

Yes, you can ask for prosperity to flow to you. But the better way I have found is to empower yourself to create more income. In this way you're *not* just asking for a handout.

Instead, you place energy into yourself to create inner change. That's where the real magick happens, and this creates the most benefit for you.

Why do I say this? *To change yourself is to change your world.*

We perceive the world around us. We can see a world of

roadblocks or *we can see opportunity*. It's our choice.

Below I'll share a ritual called *New Years Prosperity/Opportunity Ritual,* in which you'll be able to exercise your choice.

About Bathing Before Doing a Ritual

Always bathe before doing a ritual. Some ask, "Can I take a shower?" If you do not have a bathtub and only have a shower, you can still soak the herbs (I specify them below) in a large bucket of warm water.

If you take a shower, you can clear the debris of the day off first. Then, you have a choice: a) you can pour the herbs-water of the bucket upon yourself or b) you can use a cloth and wash your body with the herbs-water.

Let's Talk About Herbs For Your Ritual Bathing

Shampoo* and soap* preferably herb-infused form the best choice. Wiccans use lavender to help sooth and calm themselves to get their head in the right space.

(* Prior to your ritual bathing, Cast Circle and then cleanse and consecrate your shampoo and soap. Only use these specific items of shampoo and soap for ritual bathing.)

For a Ritual Bath, Prepare a Sachet

To prepare a sachet, begin with a 4×4 inch square piece of cheesecloth and some string to close it. *Use these Bath Herbs: Basil, Ginger and Pomegranate.* Place the bath herbs into the middle of the cloth. Then pull up the four corners of your cloth and tie them together using the string. If you don't have cloth, you can also use a clean sock or stocking that hasn't been used before.

Next draw the water for the ritual bath and place the sachet in the water. If you desire, light some candles and burn some incense.

Soak in the bath while meditating on the blessings you want to manifest in the calendar New Year. (Avoid getting stuck in thinking that you don't know how you will accomplish your desires in the everyday world.) Imagine the spiritual strength building up in you to manifest the blessings while envisioning any negative energy being soaked up by the herbs. Know you have the power to accomplish your dreams. Again, never mind the how. *The Gods will provide "the how."*

Do your part and invite the Gods to guide you in how you can make a bigger and/or better contribution and thus expand your income.

The New Years Prosperity/Opportunity Ritual

What you will need:

- Three Candles (one each: yellow, green, purple)
- Candle dressing oil (Virgin Olive oil that has been blessed and consecrated will do fine.)
- Working tools
- Altar
- Cakes and Wine

Cast circle in the usual manner.
Light the yellow candle as you say:

My eyes were once shut,

I now make them open.
Eyes that did not see,
I now have vision.
I call upon you,
the four elements of Wicca

Make the sign of the pentagram on your body [by touching your forehead followed in order: the left breast, right shoulder, left shoulder, right breast and back to forehead].

Light the Green candle and say:

Earth for fertility of my own mind
Air for new beginnings in rapid time
Fire to move the direction I must go
And
Water to birth new opportunities for me to grow

Finally light the Purple candle and say:

I call upon the Earth and Sky
I call upon the Sun and Moon
May the power to change my fate be my boon

Make the sign of the pentagram again and say:

By year's end may this take place,
for the good of all, I now claim my space.
I charge myself, my life, by the Gods' grace;
Fill me with light so my desires take place.

Do the Cakes and Wine Ceremony

Close Circle

* * *

May you and the Gods manifest the best for you in this calendar New Year.

Goddess Reveals Your Enchanted Light
Nurture Your Enchanted Light #9

Meditation Magick Exercise for Letting Go and Finding Your Hidden Strength

Have you heard that a spiritual person needs to learn how to let go and get to a place of inner peace? That sounds like a tall order. First we'll start with definitions of two forms of strength:

The Strength of Anger – in the short term, this can get us moving and it can be a channel for our own pain. But in the long term, it can lead to faulty decision-making. It is short sighted. Further, it can cause significant health problems.

The Enduring Strength of Inner Peace – Inner peace is an ever-renewing source of energy.

As my editor suggested, *"If you get your inner energy right you can do more right. Inner peace can help you get past the sorrow and the anger so you can be in the present moment and have all of your resources."*

The below meditation-exercise is not about denying the need for justice and more protection.

The below meditation-exercise is designed to empower you to stay in a place of awareness and strength.

Meditation Magick Exercise for Letting Go and Finding Your Hidden Strength

You will need:
- a blue candle
- extra virgin olive oil
- boline
- incense
- salt
- water

Cast Your Circle in your usual manner.

Cleanse your blue candle with the elements Earth and Water. Then consecrate the blue candle with your incense smoke.

Use your boline and write (on the blue candle) the name of the event that is causing your pain.

Use the olive oil to "dress your candle."

Concentrate on the blue color, which is for healing.

Light the blue candle and focus on its flame, representing the healing truth of love and strength.

Meditate on the flame. In your mind's eye, see the flame burning away all the negativity in your aura and the space around you. Once you feel your space/aura is cleansed, go to the next step …

Now imagine the pain of the event in your life. The event may be a personal experience or a public one like the Paris attacks. Create an image (in your mind) that represents the event. See the image floating above the flame. Concentrate on the image until it is a solid image above the candle. Feel it; know it is there.

Breathe deeply in and out, in and out. In your mind's eye, lower the image into the flame and watch it burn away. Feel the heat in your heart as the image and related pain is transformed into the purity of peace and strength. As the image vanishes, see that all that remains is a phoenix of peace and strength.

Do the Cakes and Wine Ceremony.

Close Your Circle in your usual way.

[When you're done with the exercise, have the candle continue burning. Make sure that things are safe so that the candle can burn until it goes out on its own. Never leave a burning candle unattended.]

I hope this meditation-exercise supports you in your personal journey of healing.

Goddess Reveals Your Enchanted Light
Nurture Your Enchanted Light #10

Blockage Release Ritual

Some people have a blockage to receiving money or love.
This following Blockage Release Ritual often helps dissolve that which blocks your highest good.

You will need:
- An object that represents the blockage in your life
- A red string or piece of yarn long enough so you can both encircle your waist and then tie the "blockage object" to you. Have at least one foot of length between you and the object.
- A boline and other ritual tools. (See my blog article at http://bit.ly/1Pheqpz for more information.)

1) Cast Your Circle
(See http://bit.ly/1Pheqpz again for more information.)

2) Begin Ritual

Asperge the "blockage object." (Asperge means to sprinkle the holy water onto the object with your fingers.)

As you asperge the object say:

I cleanse and consecrate you by water and earth.

Cense the object. (Cense means to waft incense smoke over the object.)

As you cense the object, say:

I bless and charge you with air and fire.

Asperge the yarn/string while you say:

I cleanse and consecrate you by water and earth.

Cense the yarn/string as you say,

I bless and charge you with air and fire.

Take the red yarn/string in your hands, and say:

Tiny bundle of yarn/string

You are now the same as the bonds between me and [Name of Blockage].

Tie one end of the yarn/string to the object and then encircle your waist with the other end of the yarn/string, while you say:

You are the bonds that connect us now.

From me to [Name of blockage] and from [Name of blockage] to me.

Our connection is by thee.

Sit and concentrate on the bond between you both and see it as the yarn/string that now connects you and the object.

Once you have that idea firmly in mind, use the boline to

cut the yarn/string, while you see, in your mind's eye, the astral bonds being cut along with the yarn/string.

Once you complete the cut, say:

I am now free of the ties of [Name of blockage] as it is of me.
May my happiness expand on the count of three.
One
Two
Three
Blessed be.

3) Do the Cakes and Wine Ceremony
4) Close Your Circle

Goddess Reveals Your Enchanted Light
Nurture Your Enchanted Light #11

How to Bless and Consecrate an Object

"I have this cute statue I just bought, and I am going to place it on my altar," my friend Lisa said.

"Have you blessed and consecrated it yet?" I asked.

"No." said Lisa.

"It's vital to bless and consecrate an object to make it safe to use," I emphasized.

Witches often Bless and Consecrate an object, space or person. We use this process every time we cast circle.

Use holy water to Bless and Consecrate an object and thereby remove bad energies and entities. You avoid having other energies mix with your intentions. Leaving in bad energies and entities would have created chaos and undesired effects.

Below I'm going to give two highlights from the blessing and consecrating processes.

Using Holy Water*

After Casting Circle, you hold the object and sprinkle holy water upon it (the process of asperging). Say: **I cleanse you by Earth and Water**

Using Smoke Arising from Incense

Waft the object through the smoke arising from Blessed Incense. By the way, wafting the object through smoke is the process of charging the object.

As you waft the object through smoke three times, say: **I bless and consecrate you by Fire and Air**

You have made the object suitable for use in your spellwork.

(*Witches make their own holy water with three pinches of salt.)

Goddess Reveals Your Enchanted Light
Nurture Your Enchanted Light #12

A Blessing for Success and Strength

Here's a blessing that I wrote some time ago.

I call the power of the Gods and the Mighty Ones through me.
Blessed be my mind that it be clear of all distractions. Focused on its purpose.

Blessed be my eyes that they see without judgment, that they see the correct path.

Blessed be my lips that they speak with clarity, strength and truth.

Blessed be my voice that it be clear and not shake in fear.

Blessed be my heart that I always have love and

compassion for myself and others.

Blessed be my arms that they carry my burdens with strength and ease.

Blessed be my hands that they work and create steadfastly and honorably.

Blessed be my knees that they not tremble with fear.

Blessed be my feet that they do not waver, but walk on the path of light with surefootedness.

Goddess Reveals Your Enchanted Light
Nurture Your Enchanted Light #13

"I'm So Terrified to Die"

"I'm so terrified to die," wrote one of the followers of my blog.

The person went on to say, "I don't want to be like an atheist, but I'm not connecting to my soul."

My intuition gave me the idea to share this:

"To help you connect with your soul and the Gods, I would suggest you go out into the forest or even a secluded place (pick a safe place) in a park if you can't get to the forest. Then sit quietly. Notice nature around you. Listen to the sounds of nature. Now as you sit quietly ask the God and Goddess for a sign. Breathe deeply and slowly. Be still and relax.

"The sign could be as simple as seeing a bird or some other animal (domestic or wild). You might see some fallen leaves on the ground that inspire a thought or feeling in you. Perhaps, a patch of snow in a particular shape catches your eye.

"The sign does not have to come with trumpets and a parade. Most likely, it will be something small, something quiet.

"But it will be there. Take your time and just sit. Listen and witness the miracle of the world. It may take a while. I suggest resting there for 20 minutes, 45 minutes or more. You can stay as long as you wish after that.

Do this on a regular basis. Soon you may see the signs of the Gods."

Perhaps, my comments above reach something deep in you.

We Wiccans often find the God and Goddess in quiet signs found in the natural world.

I also suggest that a number of us may find the God and Goddess in a moment of creativity. Finding a connection with God and Goddess can arrive in many ways because we're all individuals. My friend Sarah says that she finds a sign when she's drawing or sketching. It's like she becomes a conduit of the Divine.

My friend Mark tells me that he discovers insights as he writes. He may be writing for ten minutes and not like what he's writing. Then, a flash of insight, and he sees something new arrive as he keeps typing. "Where did that come from?" he asks. But then he knows. The God and Goddess wanted to say something through him.

Wiccans also connect with the God and Goddess through meditation and doing ritual.

Goddess Reveals Your Enchanted Light
Nurture Your Enchanted Light #14

Use a Witches' Bottle to Protect Yourself from Negative Energies

"Agh! I got a parking ticket!" Margie said. "I did a witches' bottle."

"Did you bury it?" I asked.

"No!"

"I see," I replied.

A Witches' Bottle protects the witch from negative energies. You use an acidic liquid, and in the olden days they used urine.

Today you can use apple cider vinegar if you prefer. Add copper pins or tacks and other sharp items.

Next, you bury it about a foot deep on your property. If you don't have a yard, find an appropriate place in the woods. The important thing is: the bottle must remain undisturbed.

Here's the process: You dig the hole, place the bottle

within and then chant:

Witches' Bottle Chant

By fire I give you spirit,
By air I give you clever thought,
By water I give you my love,
By earth I give you your body.

By the East, the South, the West and the North,
Protect me now from whatever comes forth!

Be my name banefully muttered, shouted or thought,
By this witches' bottle, have the thought caught!

In the ground you now reside,
Protecting me by my side.

Part Two

Goddess Wants You to Remove Obstacles to Your Enchanted Light

Goddess Reveals Your Enchanted Light
Remove Obstacles #1

Learning to Love the Pagan Me

Goddess knows that there are **many things in this world that obscure Your Enchanted Light.** I had to claw my way through much garbage that dragged me down like quicksand.

When I was young I was called stupid, fat and more. I sucked this poison down like sugar-water. I believed those people who attacked me. I accepted every word of it. I look back and it's easy for me to judge myself that I was so gullible. I've learned that it's valuable for me *to fight that temptation towards self-condemnation.*

Still, I believed those people, including my own brother, who said I was a big fat pig even though at the time I was 113 pounds and five foot four inches tall. I believed the haters when they told me I was stupid.

That was literally wrong. I was NOT stupid. The reality was I had a learning disability. Years later, I learned that many accomplished people have had to deal with dyslexia. In fact, Dr. Harold Levinson wrote a book titled *Smart But Feeling Dumb.* I didn't learn until recently that many successful architects, lawyers, engineers and bestselling novelists had to deal with dyslexia.

Additionally, I deal with symptoms of clinical depression. I used live under two labels "depressed person" and "lazy." I was NOT lazy. Still, my symptoms could disable me and keep me confined to my bed for a day or two. And this would fall on me any time—like bad weather.

What does this have to do with my Wiccan spiritual path?

Just as several people beat on me for my size, weight and my symptoms of clinical depression, **a number of people have oppressed me because I am Pagan.**

When you're oppressed, it's hard not to be slammed on the inside. The subconscious mind can create blockages to our inner joy.

And here's where Goddess steps in.

SECRET #2: Goddess Wants You to Learn to Remove Obstacles to Expressing Your Enchanted Light

As a citizen of the United States of America, I have lived near certain individuals who have slammed hate at me. I've seen that a number of individuals in Western society spew hateful, judgmental comments (and sometimes hateful actions!) at Pagans.

Think of all the judgments thrown around. In the USA, If you are packing on a few pounds, you're called "out of control" and "fat ass." If you take time off for your family you're called "uncommitted to your job."

I live in California, and I have some friends who think that they live in an "enlightened section of the country."

Is this true?

I've seen haters (some individuals) against Pagans in California—just like I've seen haters against my lesbian and gay friends. My good friend "Joe" was gay. He, just like many Pagans, was persecuted for who he was. Joe had to leave the military for being gay—during the time of "Don't Ask; Don't Tell."

He felt he had little options for work so he got a job at a church—of all things—an anti-gay church!

He had to be silent while hearing anti-gay comments everyday. He had clinical depression and his symptoms grew worse and worse. The people he worked for kept saying they were disgusted about gay people.

These particular "religious" people think all you have to do is pray and get religion and you would be "cured." Garbage! Joe didn't chose to be gay; he was born gay.

Similarly I was *called* to be Wiccan. *I am Wiccan through and through.*

Late one night I got the call.

They had found Joe's body in his car—a *Bible* open next to him and a gun in his glove compartment. He didn't need the firearm; the pills had ended his life.

Hearing of Joe's death, my heart broke. Tears ran down my face. Why couldn't the people near him *just accept him for who he was.* He wasn't dirty or unholy. He wasn't a terrible person. **He was a loving and kind man.**

Many Pagans go through similar situations. But they usually don't have to work at a church. They could be working at a post office or a local grocery store.

Having to hide being Pagan, as many do, can be incredibly

hard, and it's a real self-esteem crusher. You can tell yourself that the haters are wrong. But *your subconscious mind is getting a beating.*

I feel special concern for Pagan teens. My friend Joe committed suicide as a 40-year old man. Think about how vulnerable teens are! I'm in my 40s and one thing that helps me is that I've survived many upsets and tough times to reach my current age.

For teens, they do *not* have a history of surviving several tough times.

Along these lines, Sable Aradia, author of *The Witch's Eight Paths of Power: A Complete Course in Magick and Witchcraft*, wrote on her blog:

"Statistically, Pagans are more likely to experience many of the risk factors (for depression) than the average population. Most of us have suffered from feeling like black sheep; those who come from homes with opposing faiths, struggle with gender identity or practice alternate lifestyles are even more likely to experience this. We tend to be working class people, whose education often outstrips our financial circumstances, leading to frustrated ambitions and debt. We are more likely than the average population to come from abusive backgrounds and suffer from neuroses or anxiety disorders."

The noted statistics are *not* theoretical to me. I earned two educational degrees. Throughout my childhood, my brother tortured me, and my parents ignored my pleas for protection. Later, when I was in the hospital, close to death, my brother visited me, but he said, "I'm not here for you. I'm here for them [our parents]." What the hell is that? Who says that to a person in her hospital bed with the affliction Idiopathic Thrombocytopenic Purpura? My spleen was destroying my platelets. Doctors told me I could bleed out. After 30 days, a surgeon solved my health crisis: He removed my spleen.

Additionally, Wicca helped me get stronger until I felt the strength to leave an abusive marriage.

My point is: Pagans have it hard. People judge us. They do not even know us. Still they follow pop culture and the horrible things some churches say.

Earlier I mentioned ...

SECRET #2: Goddess Wants You to Learn to Remove Obstacles to Expressing Your Enchanted Light

What is one of the big obstacles? It's *a pattern of thinking* that continues the suffering we Pagans feel. One of my friends shared this quote with me:

"30% of the people will love you. 30% will hate you. And 30% couldn't care less." – Gabrielle Reece

My point is that Goddess wants us to shine. And in order to shine...

We, Pagans, just need to *let go of the idea* **we're going to be accepted by "most people."**

We're Pagans. We ARE different.

Remember Goddess wants you to nurture Your Enchanted Light.

So remember 60% of the people are NOT going to be with you anyway.

To nurture Your Enchanted Light, remember this breakdown of 30-30-30. This is good to keep in mind whenever we do something. Perhaps, you're thinking of starting a new club or writing a blog. I hope you move forward and you do *not* let fear of lack of approval stop you in your tracks.

When I was growing up I focused on the *wrong 30%* of the people I encountered. All I could see was the people who disapproved of me. I followed their drivel like a crazed fanboy for their favorite subject.

Have you noticed that many of us get pulled into the ideas from those who make the most noise? Who makes the most noise?—the people who disapprove of us. The haters.

(Notice that the people who like what you're doing may tell you, but they are *not* going to express it as loudly as the ones who disapprove of you.)

Then we, Pagans, forget the other 30% that are not even thinking of us. Unfortunately they usually get lumped in with the haters. So you feel that there are more people who are against you than is true.

(Okay, I realize that those who sit idly by and let bad things happen are NOT helping.)

The haters slam their hate on Pagans and this sickness grows and grows. This poisonous soup is the toxic feast that many people feed on. No wonder we are so sick as a society.

Without this toxic nectar, many of people in Western society wouldn't know who they are.

Think of it. Ask a certain sect of Christianity (for example), Who are you? And they reply: "We are NOT like the Catholics!"

It's this habit of trying to separate from others that creates more pain and more hate.

Sometimes people *even make up stuff just to be offended.* It makes them feel special, I guess.

For example, in November 2015 there was a big scandal.

(The below section was original published on my blog

GoddessHasYourBack.com)

Remove Obstacles #2

What's Really Going On with Pagans and the "War on Christmas"?

Has Starbucks started a War on Christianity? Really?! They did it with a simple design of a cup—a red and green cup? By the way, weren't *red* and *green* considered The Christmas Colors?

Wiccans wonder about this. I mean isn't all of the Christmas decorations, nativity scenes and Christian songs during November and December enough?

And what is the big deal about saying "Happy Holidays" instead of "Merry Christmas"?

I'm not a Christian, but I've heard that Jesus, the Christ, was into love, sharing and tolerance.

I was talking with a friend about the loud bellyaching that seems to be an annual stance of some, a *certain few,* Christians. Some Christians are touting that Starbucks having plain cups of red and green is "against Christmas." How is not having snowmen and snowflakes against Christianity?

I realize that Christianity, like many religions, began with others persecuting some members.

We Pagans know about that—we remember the horror of The Burning Times! Persecution continues. I have friends who hide their Pagan beliefs because they know that their families (yes, some Christians) would disown them. My Pagan friends also know that in some parts of the USA, they would lose their jobs if their Paganism was "found out."

Again, I emphasize *just certain* Christians are making a

big deal out of Starbucks' plain cups.

It's reported that Jesus talked about love and sharing. Giving to the poor. In fact in *The Bible* (Matthew 5:44), Jesus says, "But I tell you, love your enemies and pray for those who persecute you."

Wait a minute! Failing to place Merry Christmas on a cup is **NOT** persecution. Come on, people!

So why are certain Christians shouting "war on Christmas"?

I cannot be certain. I had a conversation with some learned people. These ideas are what arose: "A number of people feel fear. Such fear may lead to greed. And such fear may lead to the need for an opponent."

We Pagans are not an opponent.

It is *not* persecution when people say "Happy Holidays" to honor that there are people in the USA who are NOT Christian: Jews, Buddhists, Pagans, Taoists, Muslims, Sikhs, Jains, Baha'is, atheists, certain scientists, philosophers, and more.

Again, Jesus the Christ, I am told, loved people, even tax collectors and prostitutes.

In the meantime, we Pagans, can lead by example.

We'll have warm hearts acknowledging that there are many spiritual paths.

We Pagans do not need to shout about people following their own journeys.

I remember this quote:

"I like your Christ, I do not like your Christians. Your Christians are so unlike your Christ." - Mahatma Gandhi

I have Christian friends. They don't shout about Starbucks cups.

I guess that's part of why they're my friends.

How does Goddess Invite Us to Nurture Our Enchanted Light When People Are Shouting "War On Christmas"?

Know who you are! Fill your mind with love. Remember you are really part of the God and the Goddess.
It's natural for you to shine.

Goddess Reveals Your Enchanted Light
Remove Obstacles #3

How Pagans Can Triumph During the Holiday Season in the USA

Have you noticed that many Pagans feel overwhelmed with the American Holiday Season? It begins with Halloween and includes Thanksgiving and Christmas. A lot of Pagans have mixed feelings about this time of year. It starts with Samhain, a Sabbat that others stole and made into Halloween.

Next, Americans celebrate Thanksgiving, which causes situations, in which *I feel, as a Pagan, truly uncomfortable.*

Although during my childhood, I was inundated with stories of Pilgrims sitting down and enjoying a meal with Native Americans, the *real story* is one of betrayal and Pilgrims' self-righteousness. When we study the actual events, related in some truthful accounts, the Pilgrims *deceived* the Native Americans. They destroyed the Native peoples.

Consider Native American Jacqueline Keeler's assessment that "Native Americans think of this official U.S. celebration [Thanksgiving, as the] survival of early arrivals in a European invasion that culminated in the death of 10 to 30 million native people."

View Jacqueline's full comment

here. http://bit.ly/1MZtEvh

This Thanksgiving I will honor my own family and I will honor the *Native People* who reached out and helped strangers. The crops that the Pilgrims brought to this land couldn't grow. So the Native Americans gave them food and taught them how to grow crops.

I will NOT be honoring the Pilgrims.

November is Native American Month. I will honor the Native Peoples of the Americas.

So what about the turkey and all the fixins'? I will still have the food but be mindful of where the food came from. As Jacqueline Keeler noted: "Since that initial sharing ["first Thanksgiving"], Native American food has spread around the world. Nearly 70 percent of all crops grown today were originally cultivated by Native American peoples. I sometimes wonder what they ate in Europe before they met us. Spaghetti without tomatoes? Meat and potatoes without potatoes? And at the "first Thanksgiving" the Wampanoags provided most of the food—and signed a treaty granting Pilgrims the right to the land at Plymouth, the real reason for the first Thanksgiving."

So as we Pagans may feel squeezed by other people pushing Halloween, Thanksgiving and Christmas around us, *let us find our personal things to honor* during the holiday season.

Honoring what is important to you is how you, as a Pagan, can triumph.

Make each holiday season a holy time for *your* reasons.

Goddess Reveals Your Enchanted Light
Remove Obstacles #4

How Pagans Can Move Beyond Depression and Anxiety during the Holiday Season

"I'm feeling low," Matilda said.

"I hear you," I replied. "Something in particular?"

"We're squeezed from all sides. All the Christmas music, the shopping, the happy couples, the family time. Hey, it was Yule!—before the Christians hijacked our season," Matilda continued.

Ever feel, as a Pagan, that you're on a small island in the middle of "Christmas-focused people"?

The holidays often create depression and anxiety in Pagans. Seeing all the decorations and good cheer may be nice. Still, we Pagans know that one of our sacred Sabbats was perverted into a consumer holiday.

One holiday season, I was sitting in a knitting group at a

yarn shop, when an older woman exclaimed, "What's all this 'happy holidays' crap? It's Christmas, damn it! It's always going to be Christmas."

I felt my hackles rise because I knew full well that in the group were a Jew, me and an Asian with parents from China. Through our diversity, we were already demonstrating that "happy holidays" was a respectful greeting at this time of year.

Why? Because in the USA, we have people of various cultures and traditions.

Long time readers of my blog know that I deal with depression symptoms. It's true that outside things like all of this tinsel and tyranny of some people pushing their religion on others can exacerbate my depression symptoms.

Getting Past Feeling Depressed

I have learned to focus on the beauty around me and what it means to me. By this I mean, I focus on this present moment. If I see a Yule tree and I enjoy its beauty, then my depression symptoms "quiet down." Who cares what others call the tree?

Pagans Feeling Anxiety during the Holidays

I have a number of Pagan friends who have to hide their faith from their Christian family and friends. Talk about anxiety! What if the Pagan lets something slip like: "Oh, yeah. I had so much fun a PantheaCon"?

Here are some of things I do to lower my anxiety levels.

I have a particular family member who works with some

people who are not open to hearing about the pagan path. So I make sure to guard my own energy before an event with that particular group. I prepare to listen and talk about things that this group is comfortable talking about.

Most importantly, I make sure to devote time with like-minded pagans so I feel safe and nurtured—and renewed in energy.

About dealing with the consumerism of the season:

I didn't participate in Black Friday. I did not run around and attempt to get big bargains. That activity has nothing to do with the true meaning of the holiday Yule, which is about honoring the birth of the God, and the return of the sun.

Pagans and Wiccans know what Yule really means.

I practice being gentle with myself about gift-giving. Sure, you can give close ones gifts. Just go easy about it.

The way to deal with depression and anxiety is to nurture yourself.

Focus on being in the present moment. Find the beauty you cherish and create your own meaning.

Goddess Reveals Your Enchanted Light
Removing Obstacles #5

Pagans Overcoming Fear

"Sometimes, it just gets to be too much to bear, you know?" Merla said. At PantheaCon, we were taking a break. She told me about how she still had to hide her pentagram necklace at family gatherings. Her family held to a strict Christian point of view. If they knew her Pagan faith, she'd be denounced and disowned.

"I could put up with losing some family members. Hell, if my father never talked to me again, that would be a relief. But losing my baby sister. That would hurt. Really bad."

I listened closely. I kept quiet mostly so that Merla could talk herself out.

Merla feared losing all contact with her sister. I could relate to fear.

Have you noticed how fear can keep us stuck?

Will Merla ever come out to her family?

Is her relationship with her sister strong enough so she

could come out just to her sister?

These are tough questions.

Maybe not coming out to her family is the right decision for Merla. I don't know.

I do know that *if you run your whole life by fear, it can really screw you up.*

In my own journey, moving through fear has been truly important.

Recently, I gave a speech. Here is the text of that speech:

"Have you ever been so scared that fear stopped you cold?

I have!

At 15 years old, I wanted to be a writer, but I had dyslexia.

Writing scared me.

Why? Because I never had regular English classes.

I was in the special Ed group.

I never learned how to break down a sentence

Or to write a "proper paragraph."

Writing scared me.

So I shut down for over 20 years and didn't do my dream.

I have 3 Big Ideas to share with you tonight.

The first one is: "You don't have to believe. You just have to act."

Let me share how this worked in my life. I have a friend who knew an Acquisitions Editor at a top publishing company. I knew the books that came from this publisher. I really wanted to write for this publisher.

This is *the dream* for a wannabe writer like me.

The one big opportunity.

So I went to their website to find out what I needed to submit to the publisher.

Under the tab "submissions" it said that I had to submit a complete manuscript of the book.

Write a whole book?!

Are you crazy? I can't even write a paragraph.

But then I had an idea. **"Just one step."**

Did I believe I could write a book. No.

What could I do? One step.

Write a paragraph.

Another step. Write a second paragraph.

Then, write a short blog post.

One more step. Write a second blog post for the second week of the blog.

One year later. 52 blog posts done.

Now, I had most of the material for a book.

What did I learn?

"JUST ONE STEP."

Just one step at a time is all I needed.

You don't have to believe; you just have to act.

Here's my *Third Big Idea* for you tonight.

I have dyslexia. Can I polish my writing on my own?
No.

So I came up with this Third Idea:

The Power of Me Expands to the Power of We.

In my case, "We" means that I write the first draft.

It's all my ideas, my content—what comes from MY heart.

Then I bring in my editor.

Then I had other team members like a fact checker and a proofreader.

So let's go over those 2 Big Ideas:

1) JUST ONE STEP
and
2) The Power of ME expands to the Power of WE.

Now, I invite you to think of something you want.

Something you want to try.

Something you want to experience.

Think of One Step in the direction of what you want.

Yes—Doing a Google Search counts!

JUST ONE STEP.

Say that with me now.

All together

JUST ... ONE ... STEP ...

I know this works.

I'm living proof. The dyslexic who has written 5 books.

And let's all remember

"The Power of ME expands to The Power of WE."

Look around.

We're all gathered tonight.

We're supporting each other.

During the networking time, you could meet someone who can help you—and you could help that person in return.

What is possible?

More than you think.

Remember:

Just One Step

and

the Power of WE.

Thank you."

* * * * * *

In my above speech, I talked about how I dealt with fear by taking small steps forward.

In your spiritual path, what small steps can you take forward? Do you wish to connect with more Pagans? You might go to Cog.org [website of Covenant of the Goddess].

Another valuable website is witchvox.com

You could also connect with me at

askawitchnow@gmail.com

If you can find your way to California, usually in February, you can attend PantheaCon.

I invite you to find other Pagans and build your own circle of support.

Witch, Pagan, Wiccan, Christian Witches — What's the Difference?

"Christian Witches?!" my friend, Megan, stamped her foot. "No way! Somebody doesn't have a clue about what a witch is!" She went on, "A witch can't be Christian!"

There's a lot of controversy and debate over the terms Wiccan, Witch, Christian Witch, and Pagan. Some people even suggest that Wiccans are not Pagans. Some Wiccans say they do not practice magick. What?!

Certain Wiccans even claim that they do not worship the Old Gods.

Name calling and criticism arise.

So who is right and who is wrong?

It's more complicated than that.

Wicca is a term coined by Gerald B. Gardner. He used this term for a male witch. He employed Wicce for a female witch. But soon the term "Wica" was used to describe the new line of witchcraft that descended from him.

So Witchcraft and Wica were one and the same at that time. The spelling changed to Wicca some time later.

As the faith was spread, people used Wicca instead of the word Witchcraft to describe themselves. Apparently, they wanted to get away from the bad connotations that went along with the word Witch. Still, when you're a practitioner, Wicca and Witchcraft are the same.

Wicca continues to be a spiritual/religious path that has incorporated the belief in the Old Gods and Magick. Witches (this refers to both male and female practitioners) are the high priests/priestesses of the Old Religion.

Wiccans use magick to create their magick-working spaces and to honor their Gods and Goddesses for positive change in their lives.

The older Traditions of Wicca still do this.

"What are The Witch Wars?" my friend, Megan, asked. It's reported that things fell apart in the 1970-1990's when a number of new people learned some of Wicca but then left before they were taught all of the secrets of the Craft (Wicca/Witchcraft). The term "Witch Wars" refers to the yelling and thrown insults between a number of groups. Were these actual wars, including violence? I have not seen reports of that. Still, the insults, gossip, and baiting did cause real trouble.

How did things go so wrong? The new people (without full knowledge of Wicca) thought they had all the knowledge. They started their own covens and began to teach many things that weren't quite right or just downright wrong.

* * *

What Is the Difference between "Witch" and "Heathen"?

Witchcraft is a term that is very specific to the region of European/English/Scottish/Ireland area. It is a geographic area where that term was and is used. And it applies only to the people that called themselves witches in that geographic location.

Heathens are not witches, for example. They do not call themselves witches. The Heathen path is generally northern Germany/Scandinavia/Sweden. These are the people of the "heath", where heather grows in the colder European region—north of the European/English/Scottish/Ireland area.

The above is about the derivation of some terms. Anyone who practices the Wiccan faith is a witch. The religion is witchcraft. We're not only referring to people from one geographic region of the world. Wicca is spreading, and all people can practice this beautiful path.

* * *

Is it true that there are Wiccans who do not practice magick?

Some people call themselves Wiccans and claim they do no magick.

Okay, wait, hold on here. How can they claim this?

Let's go back to what Wiccans do. They Cast Circle—which, in itself, is performing magick. So if you cast circle, you do magick. You're a witch.

(There are people who use magick in their religions and who do not call themselves witches, like the

Voodoo/Vodoun/Hoodoo/Santeria religions.)

Let's also take care about the spelling of "magick." Magick is pretty much the wielding of natural forces to improve one's life. (On the other hand, "stage magic" has the label, "magic"—with no "k." Stage magic is the art of performing illusions—like the work of David Copperfield. No magick is taking place!)

"Wait a minute, what about 'ceremonial magicians'?" Megan asks. Ceremonial magicians do *not* worship the Gods and Goddesses. So by definition they are not Wiccans.

* * *

So what is a Pagan?

Pagans form a larger group of individuals who do *not* practice the Abrahamic religions. The Abrahamic religions identify the patriarch Abraham, from the Old Testament of the *Bible*, the *Torah*, and the *Quran*, as the origin of their religion. So the Abrahamic religions are: Judaism, Christianity, and Islam.

Paganism was a Christian term to indicate people who came from the country. *Pagani* is a Latin term for "country dweller" as opposed to city dweller. These country dwellers tended to keep their older religions alive (even after the arrival of Christianity or Islam). At the time, certain people referred to farmers, serfs and peasants as Pagans.

Pagans include Wiccans, Asatru, Heathen, Druids, Buddhists and more.

* * *

What about Judeo-Pagans and Christian Witches?

Sigh ... Yes, there are the people who call themselves Judeo-Pagans or Christian Witches.

Stop! Above we just went through the actual definition of Pagan—in two words let's all say it: "NOT Christian." Thank you.

The Judeo/Christian God (as reported in their sacred texts) denounces Witches, Pagans, and Wiccans.

* * *

I realize that people can and do call themselves anything they want.

What we notice is that some people stop using definitions and language as others do.

What if people create their own new terms?

For example, I have a friend who coined the term "Catapult-Moment." So he can define "Catapult-Moment" as he chooses.

Still, when we're in conversation with others, let's look back and see the definitions of what we're talking about.

Sound good?

* *Thank you to my High Priestess Lady Elinore for her guidance about some details of the above section.*

Goddess Reveals Your Enchanted Light
Remove Obstacles #7

Pagans and Medication

"I heard Wiccans use drugs," Sandy said.

"Yes and no," I replied.

True, many Wiccans use wine in our Cakes and Wine ceremony. Alcohol is a drug.

Not all Wiccans use alcohol in the Cakes and Wine ceremony. Some substitute grape juice or another fruit juice. Some completely abstain from all drugs like alcohol and caffeine. Yes, even some teas are off the list.

We can't throw all Wiccans into any rigid category. Some use other natural drugs to combat ailments such as depression symptoms, arthritis, and other sources of pain. Some imbibe marijuana, for example.

It is truly up to the individual practitioner to choose what may help for medical reasons or improved quality of life.

I know some Wiccans who aim to stay away from manufactured, pharmaceutical drugs. Some Wiccans choose to imbibe natural drugs like caffeine, alcohol or marijuana.

Many Wiccans live in states where marijuana use is illegal, and they abide by local laws. They do not break the rules of the place they live in.

I take medications that help me with an occasional migraine headache and for working with my depression symptoms. I do consult my doctor and monitor the effects of the drugs. Yes, do consult a physician about the use or non-use of drugs.

I invite you to pay close attention to how you do or do not use drugs. What results are you getting? What might you want to change for the better?

Goddess Reveals Your Enchanted Light
Remove Obstacles #8

A Ritual for A Rest from Your Burdens So You Can Recover

Recently, a number of people have contacted me expressing how heavy their life burdens are. They wish for just a short time of respite—a short break so they can recover.

A Ritual for A Rest from Your Burdens So You Can Recover

Light a candle and say this prayer aloud three times.

Prayer to the God and Goddess

Grant me a respite from my burdens, I ask this of Thee, O Lord and Lady. Help me build my strength and stamina in this time of rest that You grant me, O gracious Lady and

honorable Lord. Let me recover and grow by the power of Thee. Let me gain Your strength kind Lord, and your intelligence my beauteous Lady. So when my burdens return they weigh nothing but a feather. In this I ask Your assistance.

So Mote It Be.

Now sit and meditate on the flame as you reflect on the above prayer. Feel the weight of your burdens lifted from your shoulders.

Goddess Reveals Your Enchanted Light
Remove Obstacles #9

Rite of a Departed Soul

Many Wiccans find Samhain as the time to honor our dead. Still, death can visit our lives at other times.

Wiccans' views of death and the dead are very different from the western viewpoint of death. For us death is not a thing to be feared. Many Wiccans and Pagans believe in reincarnation. This is the belief that we will be reborn again to live a new life in a new body.

When a Wiccan friend dies I like to honor them with this rite.

Rite of a Departed Soul

What you will need:
- 2 white candles (these candles will be placed on the altar)
- One white candle for each person (covener)

- 8 candles, 4 black and 4 white (these candles will go in pairs, one white and one black at each quarter point of your circle.)
- Black robes or just where black clothes (this is a funeral after all)

Place one white and one black candle at each cardinal point. Lighting the white ones when you call the quarters. (You will be lighting the black candles from these white quarter candles).

Cast your circle as usual.

Standing at the North of your altar (facing North) Take your athame draw a pentagram.

Light North black candle [from the white quarter candle you lit when calling your quarters, and then extinguish the white candle]

High Priestess:

Lord and Lady open the gates that separate our world and the word of the dead, we send "Name of Wiccan friend here" into your care and loving embrace.

Move to the East, draw a pentagram (like you did in the North) and light East black candle [from the white quarter candle and then extinguish the white candle]

Guide "name of Wiccan friend here" way; so she can enter your beautiful lands of the dead with peace and happiness.

Move to the South, draw a pentagram and light South black candle [from the white quarter candle and then extinguish the white candle]

Guide her steps so that she is received by you safely.

Move to the west, draw a pentagram and light West black candle [from the white quarter candle and then extinguish the white candle]

Help her so that her journey be free of hardship.

High Priestess extinguishes all the candles on your altar at this point.

Wait a few moments (for a moment of silence) and then relight the candles on your altar.

Everyone then goes to the East cardinal point of the circle.

High Priestess says:

We set now set aside our grief and light a path for "Name of your friend here" to enter the peaceful place you hold for the ones who have gone before.

Each person is given a white candle. They then light their candle from the altar working candle.

Then the High Priestess relights the white candles from black ones, you then put out the black ones.

Everyone holds up their candle and then repeats the following after the High Priestess.

93

High Priestess says:

Hear us Lord, Lady and Mighty Ones; "Name of Wiccan friend here" comes to you now.

Everyone extinguishes their candle and places them on the altar.

Cakes and Wine ceremony is now done.

Close circle as usual

* * * * * *

Blessings to you at any time when you need to honor dear ones who pass away.

Goddess Reveals Your Enchanted Light
Remove Obstacles #10

A Chant for the Worst Time

Recently, my family and I dealt with a tough time with elderly family members needing care and visits at the hospital.

I wrote this Chant for such tough times:

In my darkness night I flail
Goddess grant me the strength
To find grace on my trail.
Goddess sustain me with Your Light
Guide me through this night
Let me feel your Love and Might.

Goddess Reveals Your Enchanted Light
Remove Obstacles #11

Use a Special Protection Chant

When the Wheel turns to the dark time of the year, many of us feel that we need a bit of help in terms of protection.

Here is a Special Protection Chant I have written for you:

My Lovely Lady,
My gracious great Lord,
Protect me here now,
In thou great accord!

Goddess Reveals Your Enchanted Light
Remove Obstacles #12

A Spell for Getting Rid of Pests in Your Home

This is a spell to get rid of the pests that have invaded your home.

What you need:
Large quantities of
- Dried Cedar wood chips
- Dried Eucalyptus leaves
- Orange oil
- Several square pieces of blue, cotton fabric (large enough to stuff with mixed-ingredients)
- Large bowl to mix the ingredients to be placed in each sachet
- string made of natural fiber

You will be making sachets for around your home. Make

sure you have enough ingredients to make as many as you will need for your entire home. I suggest four for a small room. Increase the number of sachets for a larger room. Remember to have sachets for a closet and cabinets. Additionally, you can use the mixture in potpourri containers.

Instructions:

Cast your Circle in the usual way.

Gather your ingredients. Cleanse and consecrate them.

Place the Cedar chips and Eucalyptus leaves in the large bowl. Add five drops of the orange oil. Now mix ingredients together by stirring counter clockwise (which is known as stirring "widdershins").

Chant:
Freaky, creepy, crawly things,
Keep away from me and all my things.
Run, Run, Run go and hide!
Leave this place and from by my side!

Next gather your blue cloth squares, and fill each with some of the mixture. Tie each square closed by using the natural fiber string. Make as many as you need.

Perform the Cakes and Wine Ceremony

Close your Circle in the usual way.

Now place the sachets in your rooms. Put a sachet in each

corner of each room. Consider placing a sachet in your vacuum bag. Remember to put sachets in various places including under your bed, beneath furniture, and in closets and cabinets.

Goddess Reveals Your Enchanted Light
Remove Obstacles #13

Blessing for Protection

Have someone you want to protect? Perhaps, you're concerned about your family member or a friend. First, you need to ask the person for his or her permission for you to cast a blessing.

Once the person has granted permission, you can use this chant:

Blessing for Protection

By the Sky and Earth,
By the Sun and Moon,
By the Sea and Land,
This I do command!

By the Lady of the Moon,
By the Lord of the bright Sun,

By East, South, West, and North,
I call protection forth!

Down and from head to toe,
Throughout the day you go.
Protected you will be
Till you come back to me.

Goddess Reveals Your Enchanted Light
Remove Obstacles #14

Choose a Love Spell with Care

A number of Wiccans get themselves into trouble by trying to use a love spell on a particular person. This violates *The Wiccan Rede* of "An It Harm None. Do as You Will."
Instead, do a spell that is more general in nature.

Simple Love Spell
This is a great little spell to attract a new romantic partner to you.
What you will need:
- One Pink Candle
- Anointing Oil

Instructions:

You will be lighting a pink candle under a waxing moon, closer to a full moon is best.

Cast circle in the usual way.

Dress, cleanse and consecrate the pink candle. Set the pink candle in the middle of your altar. Use working candle to light the pink candle and simultaneously say:

My lovely Silver Lady of the Moon,
Grant me in this night my desired boon.

I call you my love, now come my way,
Come find me my love, now come and stay.

Let the pink candle burn completely out on its own.

Do the Cakes and Wine Ceremony.

Close your Circle in the usual way.

Goddess Reveals Your Enchanted Light
Remove Obstacles #15

How A Wiccan Can Relieve Worries

As a Wiccan, I have had many worries over the years, and I have found this chant to be helpful.

The Gods' Presence Chant

Though the darkness presses in,
I know the Gods' presence within.
Open the Door for my Insights' flight,
May this be solved in a fortnight.

Goddess Reveals Your Enchanted Light
Remove Obstacles #16

For Your Protection: the Insta-circle

Use this in emergencies against bad energies. It's quick and can save you from negative forces.

While you say this chant trace a circle three times around yourself deosil (clockwise) sending out energy around you.

Chant:

I now cast the circle round, round and round!
I'm now thrice protected from head to ground!

Goddess Reveals Your Enchanted Light
Remove Obstacles #17

Stepping Out of the Darkness

Recently, I was called to give a speech.
Here is the text of that speech:

"She's eight years old and she's drowning, held underwater in a swimming pool.

Yesterday, she loved running on a hilltop in Redwood City. The grass feeling cool between her toes. Yesterday, she climbed a tree.

But today, her brother holds her down, underwater. She is drowning. And he is waiting. Waiting for her to stop moving.

What does this do to a little girl?

I can tell you. My brother finally stepped away.

But the tough times didn't end there. My brother kept up his torture of me until I couldn't take it anymore.

So at 8 years old, I stepped to the edge of my bunk bed. I wrapped some yarn around my neck again and again. I stepped off my bunk bed – And I hung there for a moment— until the yarn broke.

My story is about stepping OUT of the darkness.

Sure, I've experienced dark times, but I've also experienced other things.

I once turned to a friend and said, "How many depressed people does it take to change a light bulb? None. They just sit there in the dark." [audience laughter]

I'm glad to be speaking with you today about stepping OUT of the darkness.

Along that line, I'm going to share with you the *3 Steps of Empowerment.*

The First Step is Diagnosis. When I was 11, I was diagnosed with Major Depressive Disorder—another term for this is clinical depression. Clinical Depression is not just feeling the blues. It isn't just sometimes feeling sad. It doesn't just go away like Seasonal Affect Disorder.

Clinical Depression is like having tinnitus. That's the condition where you have constant ringing in your ears. Except this situation is a horrible feeling of pain, sadness, and hopelessness. It can get so bad that death seems like the only way out. A friend of mine killed himself. He had clinical depression.

So Diagnosis is the First Step.

The Second Step is: The person must say, "I want help."

I'm using the word "say"—but the situation is really

about taking action. The depressed person needs to take action.

You and I cannot help a depressed person if they don't want help. If they won't take their meds, and if they won't show up for therapy—there's not much we can do.

I know that I have family members who want to find a "Happy button" on me. Well—I don't have a Happy button on me.

Can I borrow yours? [I address an extrovert in the audience. The audience laughs.]

As I mentioned: the Second Step is when the person says, "I want help." The depressed person has to choose it.

I wanted help. So I worked with psychiatrists and therapists. And I take appropriate medication.

The Third Step is: Maintenance.

Sometimes, I think of maintenance of my well-being as a daily fight. I have certain "weapons" to use to hold my ground against clinical depression.

First, I have a therapy animal, a cat I named Magick. I called him Magick because he makes food disappear! [audience laughter]

I love him and petting him helps me to feel better. He helps me switch to happier thoughts. I feel he takes away some of the pain.

Second, I stay active. I go out with friends when possible. I enjoy laughing with friends. I also stay active by taking daily walks with my sweetheart.

Third, I have things that I do for myself when I'm alone. Knitting and writing are great ways to help me cope.

I have shared with you the 3 *Steps of Empowerment* that mean a lot to me.

1) Diagnosis
2) The person must say "I want help."
3) Maintenance

And finally about that eight-year-old girl who felt no one cared … She is still inside me, but now I am a full grown woman.

I am here.

I care.

I will protect her."

* * * * * *

People have told me that the above is a powerful speech. Some even invite me to expand it for a TED talk.

As a Wiccan, I still feel, at times, that I must protect myself.

Do you feel the same?

How can you protect yourself from those who do not care or do not understand our Pagan path?

I've learned that I need to face reality. To this day, my parents still do not respect my Wiccan path. They never ask me questions nor hear me out.

Part of taking care of myself is to gather with like-minded people who love me.

May you find your tribe.

Goddess Reveals Your Enchanted Light
Remove Obstacles #18

Goddess, Why Did You Let this Break Me?

"That's it. I'm done," my friend, Sandra, said.

"Tell me more. I'm listening," I said.

"How could Goddess let this happen to me?" Sandra asked.

Sometimes, life hurts so much we're left a wreck.

We wonder how a kind Goddess and God would allow such terrible things to happen.

I'm not talking from theory. As I have mentioned, I have two things: clinical depression and dyslexia.

"Wasn't just one of these things enough?!" I've asked the Goddess.

In my first year of college, I heard this idea: Some Japanese artisans repair a broken vase with lacquer mixed with gold. My first thought was "What a waste of gold."

Years later, I learned of Kintsugi, the Japanese art of repairing broken pottery with lacquer mixed with powered gold, platinum or silver. Author Christy Bartlett wrote: "Not only is there no attempt to hide the damage, but the repair is literally illuminated."

Doesn't this seem counter to what we're taught to do? If we're imperfect, aren't we supposed to hide our flaws?

Flaws make us who we are. They make us unique. Just like the broken vase, each crack is a badge of honor and forms the unique composition of ourselves.

Wicca is the path of uniqueness. It molds to each practitioner's needs. We can worship whatever pantheon we want. We can make our own rituals, tailored to ourselves and our uniqueness.

Dyslexia makes it hard to read so I was taught Wicca in a truly one-on-one, mentor-to-student manner. This was a traditional approach. I find great value in that.

It's hard to say what value I've gained from dealing with depression symptoms every day. Then I think about my connection to humor. The first thing that popped in my mind is Monty Python's song "Always Look On the Bright Side of Life."

I'm often quick to thrown in a humorous comment.

Humor has a healing experience for me.

I invite you to consider:

When we get broken, the healing is what fills the crack. And that's a gift.

Goddess Reveals Your Enchanted Light
Remove Obstacles #19

What makes you different
– The Pagan Path

Recently, I was called to give a speech.

I had a surprising conclusion, and you'll see in the text of my speech below, I've had some real struggles:

"What if every sentence was a lie? What if every word you read was a betrayal. This is what it's like to have dyslexia. It is a learning disability that makes it very difficult to read. It makes it hard to decipher letters and other symbols.

My Dad has it, too. To this day my Dad mumbles under his breath, "STUPID, STUPID, STUPID!" That's all he was told as a child.

How did dyslexia affect me as a child? Going though the public school system was horrible for me. Normally a child goes though the grades 1-6 in one school.

Not me.

I went to first grade here, second over there, and third grade at another school.

It was so hard to make friends. I only made a couple of friends—but then I was torn away, forced to go to another school where I had to start over again. It was like taking a fish from one tank and then putting her into another tank. Everything's different.

Each year I had new teachers, new rules, new classmates.

When I was 15, twenty seven years ago, dyslexia crushed my dream to be a writer.

I never learned about sentence structure nor how to compose a paragraph.

I never had classes in writing because of my dyslexia. I was just pushed through: through history, science, and geography.

Dyslexia made learning very difficult. I mean—think about it: For every subject you need to read a textbook. How do you learn math without reading? How do learn science without reading?

Homework that took the average student 15 minutes took me three hours. Even so, I averaged a 3.9 GPA in high school.

It was worse when I went to college. I had a teacher whom I will call Mr. Dense. I explained my learning disability to him.

One week later, Mr. Dense said, "I don't know why you can't learn this. Why can't you learn this?!"

What? Didn't you hear me?

Oh, that's right. You're Mr. DENSE.

Again, I worked so hard.

At one point, I was working so hard at college work and a

job to earn money.

Something had to give. I did. I collapsed at work. I still can't stand to walk into a Macy's.

I survived college. Okay, I did rather well—A's and B's.

Still, somewhere in my mind, I wanted to express myself. But I didn't think I could write.

… until I worked with my first editor, who encouraged me to write a blog.

I now write every week, and people from 173 countries read my blog.

Dealing with dyslexia gave me the chance to learn patience, to never give up, and to work hard.

So I wrote my first book, with the help of editors.

I will never forget the feeling of holding a newly printed copy of my book in my hands.

More than that—I saw favorable reviews on Amazon.com

Recently, my 5th book was published.

Yes, I could express myself. And people were getting value from my writing.

So what looked impossible to me was NOT impossible—

And Mr. Dense is still an idiot."

* * *

I feel that we Pagans also have dense people around us who are misguided by the Hollywood version of witchcraft.

In thinking about my speech, I realize that there is a parallel between my living with dyslexia AND my walking my pagan path among people who shun me or shut down if anything about my pagan-life comes up.

As I wrote in my first book, *The Hidden Children of the Goddess:* "Witches are everyday people. No, we aren't green and warty. From soccer moms to construction workers, we look just like any other person. We eat breakfast, go to work or school, and have friends and family. The only difference is our faith. In short, Wiccans are The Hidden Children of the Goddess."

Still, some misguided people will remain, like Mr. Dense, in their ignorance—and they will not listen.

So we as Pagans will need to continue on our path regardless of the Mr. Dense or Ms. Dense in our life. Some friends may fall away. Some family members may drift away.

Yes, we are different. We Pagans have found our own path.

Each one of us has a different and special path.

So I encourage you to tread upon it with joy and determination.

Goddess Reveals Your Enchanted Light
Remove Obstacles #20

Depression, Suicide, and A Wiccan Path to Healing

As I mentioned earlier in this book, my friend Joe had been tossed out of a branch of the armed forces. Why? Poor performance of his duties? No! It was his sexual orientation. A couple of years later, he killed himself. Often, every month, I remember my dear friend.

None of this is a theory to me. I've attempted suicide myself. The first time—when I was 8 years old.

Wiccans acknowledge that winter is the season of death. Death does not always mean the end of life. In the Tarot, the card "Death" also means change.

I know from my own journey that feeling the urge to kill oneself is a call for change—and a call for love.

During the winter, a significant number of people struggle with seasonal affect disorder.

For many of us who are enduring difficult times now, here is a meditation from my book *Goddess Has Your Back* to help you.

Self-Love Meditation

Close your eyes.
Breathe in and out deeply . . . Relax.
Keep breathing.
Breathe out the stress of the day.
Breathe in relaxation and peace.

(Pause)

You are still aware of the light that is in the room.
Now the light begins to fade.
As it fades you feel total comfort. You feel safe and secure in the darkness.

(Short Pause)

Now, a new form of light blossoms. It surrounds and wraps you in its loving energy. This light is the light of the Gods.
It is a light of love and compassion. Take it in.
As you take this light and understanding in, you can now see through the eyes of the God and the Goddess.
You can now see yourself as They see you, pure, beautiful, whole. You are a masterpiece of Their creation. You were made with love, and you are a manifestation of Their love. You are love.
This understanding fills you.

(Pause)

With this new understanding you are now ready to return to the physical world.

You know that even though you may leave the light at this time it is never truly gone.

It's a gentle transition as the light begins to fade around you.

Slowly at first. It gets darker and darker.

As it fades you feel total comfort. You feel safe and secure in the darkness.

(Short Pause)

Then a familiar light returns, the light in the room where you started.

It gradually gets brighter and brighter.

You are back in the room. You have brought the calm and peace and happy feelings back with you.

Now, gently open your eyes.

I hope you find comfort with this meditation.

You can also meditate and ask the God and Goddess for help. Meditate on what the Gods see as a helping answer for you. Remember, the God and Goddess are always on your side.

If you're in distress, please call the Suicide Hotline at: 1 (800) 273-8255

Yes—I have attempted suicide more than once. But now my life is good. It's really worth it to endure the pain because life CAN get better.

An Interview with Moonwater

Q: When you first thought of writing the book now known as *Goddess Reveals Your Enchanted Light,* you had note "who's really to blame"—what's that about?

Moonwater: I wanted to talk about how Western society has aspects that are really twisted. My thought was that I wanted to help fellow Pagans to free themselves from the prison of oppression that comes with judgments slammed at them by certain individuals.

Q: I notice that you've shared a number of ways—in this book—of how Pagans can celebrate what's in their heart even amid cries of "War On Christmas." Do you want to add something to that?

Moonwater: Basically, I support that we Pagans focus on our spirituality and holding it within us. We know the truth. We know who we are. We don't need others to approve of us or even accurately say what we are.

I have a few quotes that mean a lot to me about this:

"I have a dream that my four little children will one day live in a nation where they will not be judged by the color of their skin, but by the content of their character." - Martin Luther King, Jr

"Small deeds done are better than great deeds planned."
- Peter Marshall

"One can never consent to creep when one feels an impulse to soar." - Helen Keller

I encourage my fellow Pagans—and myself—to soar. To step forward with inspiration from Goddess.

And about "small deeds done," it means a lot to me if I simply light a candle to the Goddess today.

Sure, I may wait to gather with my coven and hold a more elaborate ritual. But daily, small deeds mean a lot to our soul—and to Goddess.

Q: In your notes for this book, you had a comment "How can I truly see?" Would you elaborate on that?

Moonwater: Instead of looking outward and seeing what other people place on you, focus on how you see yourself and how Goddess sees you. You'll find that there's a big difference.

Q: I hear you about that. I'm still wondering how I can see myself—maybe the good part of me—that Goddess sees.

Moonwater: That takes us back to the Self-Love Meditation that I shared in this book [in the section titled

Depression, Suicide, and A Wiccan Path to Healing.]

Q: At one point, you mentioned to me that you had notes about the Tarot Card known as "The Hanged Man." How does that relate to this book?

Moonwater: To me the Hanged Man is about a change in perspective.

I once read that the Hanged Man card is about seeing opportunities to grow in unpleasant events. Much of this book is about how Pagans can persevere and even better than that—we can triumph! It's a matter of perspective and how we fill our minds in this present moment. Am I going to complain bitterly about those certain individuals who are filled with prejudice against Pagans? Or am I going to do what is necessary to strengthen myself?

In this book, I've shared my struggles with fear, dyslexia and clinical depression. It's really an encouraging message of: *If I can persist through such trouble that felt overwhelming to me, you, my friend, when you welcome Goddess' guidance can move forward.* I wish I could say to my friend Joe who killed himself: "It *does* get better!"

Goddess Reveal Your Enchanted Light
Remove Obstacles #21

The Pagan Path to Goddess AND Community

An Interview with Moonwater

Question: You began as a solitary witch—yes?

Moonwater: Yes. It was very lonely. Sure, I could practice whenever I wanted. But I didn't do it very often because of the people I was living with. I was surprised when I moved into a new neighborhood. I found other pagans. So when you feel that something is tough or painful, it's sometimes when Goddess is opening a new door for you. I remember this quote:

"When one door of happiness closes, another opens; but often we look so long at the closed door that we do not see the one which has been opened for us." - Helen Keller

So I spent some serious time missing my old life and my old place where I had lived. But then my new neighbors opened new vistas for me. For example, the first time I went to PantheaCon was with my new neighbors.

Soon we formed a small cover of just three people. That was also the first year in which I learned Tarot.

Q: What about PantheaCon? What worked for you there?

Moonwater: It really helped me because now I could see people in my community. It means a lot when you see well over 2,000 fellow Pagans all gathered together. I had come home.

Q: What was a big difference in your Pagan path from this moment forward?

Moonwater: It was definitely nice to have a mentor. Someone I could go to if I was having some problems with my spellwork or if I just had questions about life in general. What happens when we die ... other things ... the usual [smiles].

Q: What about the differences when you did spellwork?

Moonwater: In a coven there's more *power*. Different people place their energy in—it's not just you.

Q: I'm curious. With any group, some people sort of bump into each other because of differences in personalities. Have you had to work with that?

Moonwater: I've been fortunate. If any of us has had a

tough day, we do a grounding exercise BEFORE we Cast Circle.

When I act as High Priestess for the coven, I sense the energy in the room. If necessary, I have the coveners do a short grounding exercise before we start anything else.

I have them put both feet on the floor and do some belly-breathing. Sometimes, I say, "Let's all leave any cares outside of this room. If you have any tightness or tension, just imagine it as black energy and just push it down into the earth so it's harmlessly absorbed."

My coven is used this so we don't have to do such a grounding exercise often.

When we Cast Circle, we're in the place in between worlds. It's a holy place.

Being in a coven is nice because you can watch each other's backs.

Being in a coven is like being in a family.

(Do you wish to connect with more Pagans? You might go to Cog.org [website of Covenant of the Goddess].

Another valuable website is witchvox.com

You could also connect with Moonwater at askawitchnow@gmail.com

If you can find your way to California, usually in February, you can attend PantheaCon.)

A Moment for Helpful Tips
(I originally shared this material in my enewsletter.)

Love stones and crystals? Is your collection getting out of hand? You can use an old fish tackle box or bead storage box to sort and store your collection. The compartments make it easy to separate and store your stones. When you're ready to use them just pop the container open, and you have everything easily accessible and ready to go.

Fire-starters: An Easy Method to Light Your Campfire

Here is a method that I use to make it easy to start a campfire.
Please be quite careful in how you implement this.
I take my time and devote care in the below process.
When camping at a Pagan event or just camping, I make a "fire-starter," which is a handy tool to start one's campfire.

What you will need:
- Wax
- A double boiler to melt the wax in

- Cotton makeup removal pads
- Tin foil
- Tongs

Melt wax. Use the tongs to pick up a cotton makeup removal pad; then dip it into the melted wax. Place the item on tin foil to cool. Repeat this process to create a number of fire-starters.

Peel the fire-starters off the tin foil after they have dried. Done!

To use Fire-starters

Light one end of a fire-starter and place it on the wood of your campfire. That's it.

A fire-starter acts like a candle, continuing to burn for a while to get your campfire lit.

A Moment for a Helpful Tip

Many witches like to grow plants, especially for spellwork. Begin with a starter container to have the seedlings germinate. You can save funds on a starter container by picking a container that you were about to recycle. After attending a restaurant, I use a clear plastic container in which I packed my leftovers.

Clean the container and place a layer of potting soil in the bottom. Place your seeds in the soil, close the lid and place the container on a windowsill. You'll note that this is a great way to start your garden in early Spring when it's still too cold to plant your garden outside.

Make a Small Terrarium
Use a jug-style, milk container. On the side of the container, cut a small opening (like the 3 sides of a square) – and in this way make a little "door." Through the door, place potting soil at the bottom.

Using this small terrarium, you can grow bulbs. For example, one of my friends grows green onions in this manner. Just place the terrarium in direct sunlight.

You can also use a one litter soda bottle in the same way as described above.

The above options help you have a mini-greenhouse.

Good planting and harvesting.

A Moment for "Isn't That Interesting?"

Why Do We Have Yule Trees and Wreaths?

"You call them Yule trees. I grew up hearing them called Christmas trees," my friend Kevin said.

"That may be so. Still, Yule is the Winter Solstice. Yule has been celebrated for thousands of years," I replied.

Yule trees signify everlasting life. Our ancestors believed that evergreen trees were special. Why?

In the winter time, all the vegetation of the land died, except for evergreen trees. These trees defied death. These trees held some special power against Winter.

Realize that Winter was a scary and tough time for our ancestors. Vegetation perished and people died due to cold, illness and lack of food.

Our ancestors held the evergreen tree—the Yule Tree—as a sign of life in the middle of Winter ... and as a symbol of eternal life.

Our ancestors brought evergreen trees into the home to

bring this energy to the people who dwelled there.

When made into wreaths the combination of the circle (the Circle of Life) and the evergreens made the symbol of everlasting life all that more potent.

I invite my fellow Pagans to smile when they see Yule Trees.

We know the special meaning and we can celebrate that!

Goddess Reveals Your Enchanted Light
Remove Obstacles #22

Support Your Inner Peace in a World of Voices Arguing Over Deity

Have you caught a bit broadcast news and heard about someone's cruelty to another person—and it bothered you?

Or maybe you've wondered about how some extremists use religion as a justification for terrible acts.

Recently, just as I was drifting off to sleep, an idea blazed across the expanse of my mind.

Picture this. **Deity is water. Each human being is a vessel.**

Imagine that Deity's essence as a large infinite ball of water.

Let's say you're a bowl and you grow up among bowls. All you know are bowls. In fact, you might say that bowl people have "bowl Gods" because they see themselves in what they picture to be Divine.

On the other side of the ocean are goblets. And they only

know themselves as goblets. So they have "goblet Gods."

But Deity fills ALL bowls and ALL goblets. Deity is ONE. Deity is in everyone.

Water will take the shape of any vessel it fills. The vessels may differ dramatically, but what fills them is the same.

Ideally, we Pagans get a glimpse of the essence of Deity. All who see Deity, see the Source and realize the Source is just dressed in the garb inspired by various cultures.

(We're talking about the form *water*. Certainly, Deity can take any form: water, vapor or solid. By the way, we Pagans know that we can relate to Gods and Goddesses that we choose. In essence, Deity has different forms and we can connect with the form that moves our heart.)

Our problem, that is human beings' problem, is that we see ourselves as vessels—as bowls or goblets.

Do we humans get caught up in looking at vessels? Sure we do. Research reveals that tall people and "pretty" people get treated better than others. They get the jobs and the promotions.

You could even extend this metaphor of Deity as water to other galaxies.

Astrophysicist Neil Degrasse Tyson once said, "My great fear is that we've in fact been visited by intelligent aliens, but they chose not to make contact, on the conclusion that there's no sign of intelligent life on Earth."

My point is that this metaphor of Deity as water applies to the thought that *Deity is in* such possible aliens. Instead of goblets or bowls, such aliens could be buckets. I'm just saying.

My metaphor of Deity is water applies to all life and all matter.

Neil Degrasse Tyson has talked about dark matter which relates to 85% of the gravity in the universe. "Dark matter. I get asked what it is. And my best answer is we haven't a clue. We don't know what it is," Tyson said.

I will suggest that Deity is dark matter, too.

In any case, when you hear about someone who is ignorant about Paganism spouting dumb theories, see if you can allow that Deity is water. There is some Deity in that other person. What is the big difference? That person is probably *shut down* in some way. He or she does not hear the inspiration from Goddess—which is that person's loss.

So maybe you can muster a bit of compassion to send in that direction.

Some spiritual paths suggest: Love everyone.

I do like the idea that it's sometimes good to love toxic people from afar!

YOUR PATH CONTINUES

As we complete this journey with this book, I celebrate your efforts and spiritual growth.

Please continue your journey with me by viewing my articles at my blog at GoddessHasYourBack.com

Additionally, learn rituals, chants, tips, and ways to customize your rituals just for you ... and even more when you sign up for my exclusive enewsletters. Just go to GoddessHasYourBack.com and click on the link (on the right side of the webpage).

Blessed Be,
Moonwater SilverClaw

ABOUT THE AUTHOR

Moonwater SilverClaw is a Wiccan High Priestess and member of the Covenant of the Goddess and the New Wiccan Church. She has trained people new to Wicca. Her personal story reveals how Wicca saved her life and helped her strengthen herself to secure her release from an abusive marriage.

Moonwater has been practicing Wicca since 1990, first as a solitary and then in a coven.

Moonwater posts at her blog,

GoddessHasYourBack.com

[with visitors from 173 countries]

She felt called to write the blog even through she is dyslexic. She works with a team of editors. She says, "I wish to educate those who don't understand what the Craft is about. Some people may not yet identify themselves as Pagan, but they'd like more information."

Moonwater has addressed college students in Comparative Religion classes for over ten years. She leads workshops. She lives with her cat Magick and her sweetheart of many years; he is one of her editors. She enjoys knitting and photography.

Her work is endorsed by Wiccan notables including Patrick McCollum (receiver of the Mahatma Gandhi Award for the Advancement of Religious Pluralism).

Moonwater SilverClaw can be contacted at:

AskAWitchNow@gmail.com

Or at her blog:

GoddessHasYourBack.com

Special Offer Just for Readers of this Book:

Contact Moonwater SilverClaw at askawitchnow@gmail.com for special discounts on books, coaching, workshops and presentations. Just mention your experience with this book.

Excerpt from
Goddess Has Your Back

by Moonwater SilverClaw

CHAPTER 1:
GODDESS HAS YOUR BACK

Would you like your Wiccan path to lift up your self-esteem?

Would you simply like to feel better?

This book helps you actually feel your connection with the Goddess on a daily basis—even moment to moment.

As I mentioned in my first two books, *The Hidden Children of the Goddess* and *Beyond the Law of Attraction to Real Magick,* Wicca saved my life and empowered me to leave an abusive marriage.

As a High Priestess, I have supported friends, family, and colleagues in times of need. My blog TheHiddenChildrenoftheGoddess.com gives me a weekly opportunity to support website visitors from over 173 countries.

This book gives *us* the space and time to really explore magickal practices, rituals, meditations and experiences that you'll find comforting and uplifting.

My journey upon this path began with meeting the Gods. The Gods showed me the true path to self love and acceptance. Where I saw nothingness and unworthiness, they showed me abundance and a unique specialness that I had.

Now I will let you in on a secret. *You have your own unique specialness that no one else has.* It is yours, and yours alone.

This new path is yours to discover and walk. Just like my own path, your path is a beautiful discovery simply waiting for you. Prepare to step forward on this new, wondrous, and beautiful path.

Let's take the next step.

Secret of How to Do Magick

When I first started doing magick it was really hit or miss, most often *mess*. My spell work was just not as effective as I wanted it to be. What was I doing wrong?

If you have wondered the same thing, you have probably done similar mistakes. For example, I'd do a money spell, but I'd just get new problems!

The real problem was, like many people, I just wanted a big payday. What I didn't know was that this is really the wrong way to approach a lack of money.

Many, if not most, spells written today are focused on the external opportunities or even requesting gifts from the Gods. Focusing on just the external can create new problems.

What if I could tell you a **Secret of how to do magick**—in a way where you avoid ethics issues about money?

I have mentored a number of people about this *Secret*. Now I will share with you this Secret.

A phrase from the poem by Doreen Valiente entitled *The Charge of the Goddess* tells us how to do magick well. But many of us, like my younger self, just don't see it. The line I'm talking about is: "...if that which thou seekest thou findest not within thee, thou wilt never find it without thee."

This line invites us to look within as we approach our magickal work.

Instead of focusing on how to get money from outside sources, focus within. How? Instead of asking for a handout from the universe, ask, **"How I can create more energy in** myself to obtain my desire? How can I make myself open to more prosperity?"

Let's get more specific. You have been laid off and need a new job pronto! Bills are pilling up fast.

Let's use a sigil for this purpose.

How to Make Your Own Personal Sigils

Imagine putting a magical intention into an object. Why would you do that? Wiccans do this because they want the object to hold power to help them realize a personal desire. For example, you may be job hunting and you want the power of the object—in this case, a sigil—to assist you to get the ideal job.

Making your own personal sigils is easy. Some time ago, author/artist Austin Osman Spare devised a method for creating sigils.

Since that time, a number of authors have discussed Austin Osman Spare's process of making sigils. One book I appreciate is Frater U. D.'s *Practical Sigil Magic: Creating Personal Symbols for Success.*

I have made a couple of my own additions to the process.

First, throughout history, witches made sigils out of virgin parchment. But that is quite expensive. Also if you're vegan and will not wear leather, you will want to use something else. Why? Parchment is typically made from sheep skin. So let's talk about a process devoid of parchment.

I use the heavier art paper, the kind that absorbs ink and which can be infused with different tinctures made with herbs. Watercolor paper is a nice choice, too.

What about inks? You could use one of the many magickal inks on the market. My favorite is Dragons Blood Ink. But magickal inks can be expensive. So you can make your own out of a high grade ink such as Winsor Newton ink or India ink. To make it a magickal ink just add some essential oil to it, like myrrh. Mix and consecrate.

You can even use Sharpie pens as author Peter Paddon suggests. Just make sure to designate specific pens for only magickal work. They'll be part of your set of magickal tools.

You can use different colors for different desires. Here is a short list of colors and meanings that I include in my book *The Hidden Children of the Goddess:*

- Red: sex, desire, vitality, strength
- Orange: charm, confidence, joy, persuasion
- Yellow: intellectual development, joy, intellectual strength
- Green: prosperity, abundance, fertility, money matters
- Blue: healing, protection, spiritual development
- Purple: the occult, power, magick
- Pink: love, friendship, compassion
- White: purity, innocence, peace, tranquility

Write out your desire on a scratch piece of paper; you can use a single word or a phrase. Some examples are:

- I want an ideal job for me at this time
- Happiness
- I need a new house
- Success

We'll now use the word "Success" as our example. Cross off all of the repeat letters in Success. You end up with S, U, C, and E. (You want only one of each letter that appears in the word.) Next, scramble the letters, getting S, E, U, and C (for example).

Now comes the fun part: Combine the letters together in

an image.

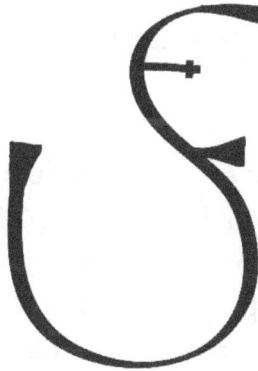

Success Sigil

Can you find the letters?

In this way you can make all sorts of sigils.

If you want to imbue it with a potion or tincture, this is the time to do it. You can either soak the paper in your tincture or brush it on. Either way you must let it dry. Overnight is best.

Now with this new image (of combined letters), inscribe it with your magical ink on your absorbent paper.

Now that you have the sigil, the next step is to breathe life into it with Pranic Breathing, also known as belly breathing. If you're familiar with yoga, you are probably familiar with Pranic Breathing techniques. Breathe in deeply; allow your stomach to inflate. Visualize pulling up energy from the earth. When you have built up enough energy in your lungs, blow it onto the sigil. This will charge it with your energy and further empower your intention.

Now place your sigil in a safe place and forget about it. Forgetting about it is the toughest part of the whole process. This helps the magick work.

As you can see, making your own sigils is quite easy and fun. After some practice, you will be able to do them quickly and easily.

Remember the Gods are here to help. You can call on them for inner strength.

How to phrase a sentence for a sigil to get a job:

- All blocks I have put up, known and unknown, dissolve so that I am a good candidate and my future employer hires me.
- Help me express the inner strength, skills and energy so that I can acquire a job of my liking.

Here are phrases for those who have an interest in an entrepreneurial path:

- I find new ways to serve others successfully so that money comes to me naturally.
- All blocks I have put up, known and unknown, dissolve so that I can create abundance in my life.

Can you see how each sentence or phrase focuses on inner change, not the external "give me, give me"? With these phrases you are not looking for a handout. **You are creating the abundance by changing *yourself*.**

This can be applied to the rest of your magick as well. Another example is love spells. Focus your magick on *being more loving, or more open to love.* Never do love spells *upon* a particular person. Instead do a spell to attract love to you in whatever form is appropriate by creating yourself as more loving.

By focusing on inner change and developing our inner strengths, we can achieve our desires.

Goddess Has Your Back in the Worst Times

When you're reading a book what are you looking for? I'm looking for the truth and some way to become stronger. I promise to provide both for you in this chapter.

END OF EXCERPT
from *Goddess Has Your Back*
Available from Amazon.com

* * * * * *

See the next page for an **Excerpt from *Beyond the Law of Attraction to Real Magic* by Moonwater SilverClaw**

Excerpt from *Beyond the Law of Attraction to Real Magic* by Moonwater SilverClaw

Beyond the Law of Attraction to Real Magick
How You Can Remove Blocks to Prosperity, Happiness and Inner Peace

Self-perspective: Overcome the Blockage of Not Feeling Worthy

Do you feel worthy of the best that life has to offer? Maybe on the conscious level you say, "Sure. Bring it on. The new house, new car, and a real, loving relationship."

But have you ever sabotaged your chances of getting exactly what you wanted?

Self-sabotage can occur because of feeling not worthy on a subconscious level.

If it's subconscious, how can we deal with this?

Good question.

Soon I will share with you a Self-Love Meditation.

But first let's talk about magick. The whole premise of this book is that there is a way to go about the Law of Attraction with more power.

To put it simply, the Law of Attraction is a form of magick, but people who read an introductory book on the Law of Attraction are often denied enough information to truly make the Law of Attraction work in their own lives.

So to really make a positive difference in your life, we need to talk about real magick. I spell magick with a "k" to distinguish it from stage magic you see on television.

Magick is a natural power, *not* a supernatural one. Who uses magick? In my spiritual path, Wicca, one is trained to use magick in appropriate ways.

When Wiccans do magick, they channel *natural* energies and create change with them.

Well, if Wicca isn't really supernatural, then why practice Wicca at all?

To put it simply, *you want something.* That's probably why you were interested in the Law of Attraction in the first place. Now in the context of learning real magick, you'll be able to fully use the Law of Attraction. And that's good news!

Everyone is different and has their own answer to that question. I like to think of religion as a bottle of wine. Let's say you have three different people who all taste the same bottle of wine. The first person points out that the flavor has accents of oak. The second praises the hints of apple in it, and the third enjoys the floral notes. They are all right. The wine contains all the flavors they described. But each person detected something different. Religion is like that. Deity can't be entirely known. So the truth of it is scattered into many faiths.

In Wicca, we honor the God and the Goddess. If that's new to you, you can substitute the label of Higher Power or God or Deity.

The Gods and Goddesses have helped me and they can help you, too. The first thing they taught me was self-love.

Before we go further, let's make a distinction between self-love and self-conceit (or being stuck in one's ego).

Self-love is about kindness and support. So it's a good thing. It is NOT about your ego or puffing yourself up.

Let me show you how the Gods changed my perspective on myself for the better.

One of the best exercises I learned is meditation. Through reflective meditation, the Gods helped me understand how skewed my perception of myself really was. This was a key turning point for me.

One thing you always hear about are affirmations, but for many of us these just don't work.

First, let's cover what an affirmation is. It's a personal, positive statement. It can be as simple as "I feel terrific" or "I make a lot of money."

For many, the above statements don't work. Why?

A number of people have said, "It just sounds like I'm lying to myself."

Like myself, many people's inner self-beliefs interfere with these positive statements. For an example, if I used the affirmation "I am thin," my brain would object with "No, I'm not. Look in the mirror." It's not true. No matter how hard you try to pound that new idea into your brain, your brain pounds just as hard back.

So how did the Gods help me deal with this problem? They inspired me to create a Self-Love Meditation.

So instead of the uphill battle of an affirmation, we'll use the Self-Love Meditation to work with the situation.

END OF EXCERPT
from *Beyond the Law of Attraction to Real Magick*

Purchase your copy of the above books (paperback or ebook) at
Amazon.com or BarnesandNoble.com
See **Free Chapters** of Moonwater SilverClaw's 5 books
at http://amzn.to/1tni9WP

www.ingramcontent.com/pod-product-compliance
Lightning Source LLC
LaVergne TN
LVHW051239080426
835513LV00016B/1678